Ballads of a Cheechako

BY
ROBERT W. SERVICE

Author of
"The Spell of the Yukon"

NEW YORK
BARSE & HOPKINS
PUBLISHERS

CONTENTS

7

CONTENTS

CONTENTS

TO THE MAN OF THE HIGH NORTH

My rhymes are rough, and often in my rhyming
   I've drifted, silver-sailed, on seas of dream,
Hearing afar the bells of Elfland chiming,
   Seeing the groves of Arcadie agleam.

I was the thrall of Beauty that rejoices
   From peak snow-diademed to regal star;
Yet to mine aerie ever pierced the voices,
   The pregnant voices of the Things That Are.

The Here, the Now, the vast Forlorn around us;
   The gold-delirium, the ferine strife;
The lusts that lure us on, the hates that hound us;
   Our red rags in the patch-work quilt of Life.

The nameless men who nameless rivers travel,
   And in strange valleys greet strange deaths alone;
The grim, intrepid ones who would unravel
   The mysteries that shroud the Polar Zone.

These will I sing, and if one of you linger
   Over my pages in the Long, Long Night,
And on some lone line lay a calloused finger,
   Saying: "It's human-true—it hits me right;"
Then will I count this loving toil well spent;
Then will I dream awhile—content, content.

MEN OF THE HIGH NORTH

Men of the High North, the wild sky is blazing;
  Islands of opal float on silver seas;
Swift splendors kindle, barbaric, amazing;
  Pale ports of amber, golden argosies.
Ringed all around us the proud peaks are glowing;
  Fierce chiefs in council, their wigwam the sky;
Far, far below us the big Yukon flowing,
  Like threaded quicksilver, gleams to the eye.

Men of the High North, you who have known it;
  You in whose hearts its splendors have abode;
Can you renounce it, can you disown it?
  Can you forget it, its glory and its goad?
Where is the hardship, where is the pain of it?
  Lost in the limbo of things you've forgot;
Only remain the guerdon and gain of it;
  Zest of the foray, and God, how you fought!

12

MEN OF THE HIGH NORTH

You who have made good, you foreign faring;
   You money magic to far lands has whirled;
Can you forget those days of vast daring,
   There with your soul on the Top o' the World?
Nights when no peril could keep you awake on
   Spruce boughs you spread for your couch in
      the snow;
Taste all your feasts like the beans and the bacon
   Fried at the camp-fire at forty below?

Can you remember your huskies all going,
   Barking with joy and their brushes in air;
You in your parka, glad-eyed and glowing,
   Monarch, your subjects the wolf and the bear?
Monarch, your kingdom unravisht and gleaming;
   Mountains your throne, and a river your car;
Crash of a bull moose to rouse you from dreaming;
   Forest your couch, and your candle a star.

You who this faint day the High North is luring
   Unto her vastness, taintlessly sweet;
You who are steel-braced, straight-lipped, enduring,
   Dreadless in danger and dire in defeat:
Honor the High North ever and ever,
   Whether she crown you, or whether she slay;
Suffer her fury, cherish and love her—
   He who would rule he must learn to obey.

MEN OF THE HIGH NORTH

Men of the High North, fierce mountains love you;
    Proud rivers leap when you ride on their breast.
See, the austere sky, pensive above you,
    Dons all her jewels to smile on your rest.
Children of Freedom, scornful of frontiers,
    We who are weaklings honor your worth.
Lords of the wilderness, Princes of Pioneers,
    Let's have a rouse that will ring round the
       earth.

THE BALLAD OF THE NORTHERN LIGHTS

One of the Down and Out—that's me. Stare at
    me well, ay, stare!
Stare and shrink—say! you wouldn't think that
    I was a millionaire.
Look at my face, it's crimped and gouged—one of
    them death-mask things;
Don't seem the sort of man, do I, as might be the
    pal of kings?
Slouching along in smelly rags, a bleary-eyed, no-
    good bum;
A knight of the hollow needle, pard, spewed from
    the sodden slum.
Look me all over from head to foot; how much
    would you think I was worth?
A dollar? a dime? a nickel? Why, *I'm the wealth-*
    iest man on earth.

No, don't you think that I'm off my base. You'll
    sing a different tune
If only you'll let me spin my yarn. Come over to
    this saloon;

15

BALLAD OF THE NORTHERN LIGHTS

Wet my throat—it's as dry as chalk, and seeing as
    how it's you,
I'll tell the tale of a Northern trail, and so help me
    God, it's true.
I'll tell of the howling wilderness and the haggard
    Arctic heights,
Of a reckless vow that I made, and how *I staked
    the Northern Lights*.

Remember the year of the Big Stampede and the
    trail of Ninety-eight,
When the eyes of the world were turned to the
    North, and the hearts of men elate;
Hearts of the old dare-devil breed thrilled at the
    wondrous strike,
And to every man who could hold a pan came the
    message, "Up and hike."
Well, I was there with the best of them, and I knew
    I would not fail.
You wouldn't believe it to see me now; but wait
    till you've heard my tale.

You've read of the trail of Ninety-eight, but its
    woe no man may tell;
It was all of a piece and a whole yard wide, and the
    name of the brand was "Hell."
We heard the call and we staked our all; we were
    plungers playing blind,

BALLAD OF THE NORTHERN LIGHTS

And no man cared how his neighbor fared, and no
    man looked behind;
For a ruthless greed was born of need, and the
    weakling went to the wall,
And a curse might avail where a prayer would fail,
    and the gold lust crazed us all.

Bold were we, and they called us three the "Unholy
    Trinity;"
There was Ole Olson, the sailor Swede, and the
    Dago Kid and me.
We were the discards of the pack, the foreloopers
    of Unrest,
Reckless spirits of fierce revolt in the ferment of
    the West.
We were bound to win and we revelled in the hard-
    ships of the way.
We staked our ground and our hopes were crowned,
    and we hoisted out the pay.
We were rich in a day beyond our dreams, it was
    gold from the grass-roots down;
But we weren't used to such sudden wealth, and
    there was the siren town.
We were crude and careless frontiersmen, with
    much in us of the beast;
We could bear the famine worthily, but we lost our
    heads at the feast.

BALLAD OF THE NORTHERN LIGHTS

The town looked mighty bright to us, with a bunch
    of dust to spend,
And nothing was half too good them days, and
    everyone was our friend.
Wining meant more than mining then, and life was
    a dizzy whirl,
Gambling and dropping chunks of gold down the
    neck of a dance-hall girl;
Till we went clean mad, it seems to me, and we
    squandered our last poke,
And we sold our claim, and we found ourselves one
    bitter morning—broke.

The Dago Kid he dreamed a dream of his mother's
    aunt who died—
In the dawn-light dim she came to him, and she
    stood by his bedside,
And she said: "Go forth to the highest North till
    a lonely trail ye find;
Follow it far and trust your star, and fortune will
    be kind."
But I jeered at him, and then there came the Sailor
    Swede to me,
And he said: "I dreamed of my sister's son, who
    croaked at the age of three.
From the herded dead he sneaked and said: 'Seek
    you an Arctic trail;

BALLAD OF THE NORTHERN LIGHTS

'Tis pale and grim by the Polar rim, but seek and
    ye shall not fail.' ''
And lo! that night I too did dream of my mother's
    sister's son,
And he said to me: "By the Arctic Sea there's a
    treasure to be won.
Follow and follow a lone moose trail, till you come
    to a valley grim,
On the slope of the lonely watershed that borders
    the Polar brim."
Then I woke my pals, and soft we swore by the
    mystic Silver Flail,
'Twas the hand of Fate, and to-morrow straight
    we would seek the lone moose trail.

We watched the groaning ice wrench free, crash on
    with a hollow din;
Men of the wilderness were we, freed from the
    taint of sin.
The mighty river snatched us up and it bore us
    swift along;
The days were bright, and the morning light was
    sweet with jewelled song.
We poled and lined up nameless streams, portaged
    o'er hill and plain;
We burnt our boat to save the nails, and built our
    boat again;

BALLAD OF THE NORTHERN LIGHTS

We guessed and groped, North, ever North, with
  many a twist and turn;
We saw ablaze in the deathless days the splendid
  sunsets burn.
O'er soundless lakes where the grayling makes a
  rush at the clumsy fly;
By bluffs so steep that the hard-hit sheep falls
  sheer from out the sky;
By lilied pools where the bull moose cools and wal-
  lows in huge content;
By rocky lairs where the pig-eyed bears peered at
  our tiny tent.
Through the black canyon's angry foam we
  hurled to dreamy bars,
And round in a ring the dog-nosed peaks bayed to
  the mocking stars.
Spring and summer and autumn went; the sky
  had a tallow gleam,
Yet North and ever North we pressed to the land
  of our Golden Dream.

So we came at last to a tundra vast and dark and
  grim and lone;
And there was the little lone moose trail, and we
  knew it for our own.
By muskeg hollow and nigger-head it wandered
  endlessly;

BALLAD OF THE NORTHERN LIGHTS

Sorry of heart and sore of foot, weary men were
we.
The short-lived sun had a leaden glare and the
darkness came too soon,
And stationed there with a solemn stare was the
pinched, anaemic moon.
Silence and silvern solitude till it made you dumbly
shrink,
And you thought to hear with an outward ear the
things you thought to think.

Oh, it was wild and weird and wan, and ever in
camp o' nights
We would watch and watch the silver dance of the
mystic Northern Lights.
And soft they danced from the Polar sky and swept
in primrose haze;
And swift they pranced with their silver feet, and
pierced with a blinding blaze.
They danced a cotillion in the sky; they were rose
and silver shod;
It was not good for the eyes of man—'twas a sight
for the eyes of God.
It made us mad and strange and sad, and the gold
whereof we dreamed
Was all forgot, and our only thought was of the
lights that gleamed.

BALLAD OF THE NORTHERN LIGHTS

Oh, the tundra sponge it was golden brown, and
    some was a bright blood-red;
And the reindeer moss gleamed here and there like
    the tombstones of the dead.
And in and out and around about the little trail
    ran clear,
And we hated it with a deadly hate and we feared
    with a deadly fear.
And the skies of night were alive with light, with a
    throbbing, thrilling flame;
Amber and rose and violet, opal and gold it came.
It swept the sky like a giant scythe, it quivered
    back to a wedge;
Argently bright, it cleft the night with a wavy
    golden edge.
Pennants of silver waved and streamed, lazy ban-
    ners unfurled;
Sudden splendors of sabres gleamed, lightning
    javelins were hurled.
There in our awe we crouched and saw with our
    wild, uplifted eyes
Charge and retire the hosts of fire in the battle-
    field of the skies.

But all things come to an end at last, and the
    muskeg melted away,
And frowning down to bar our path a muddle of
    mountains lay.

BALLAD OF THE NORTHERN LIGHTS

And a gorge sheered up in granite walls, and the
    moose trail crept betwixt;
'Twas as if the earth had gaped too far and her
    stony jaws were fixt.
Then the winter fell with a sudden swoop, and the
    heavy clouds sagged low,
And earth and sky were blotted out in a whirl of
    driving snow.

We were climbing up a glacier in the neck of a
    mountain pass,
When the Dago Kid slipped down and fell into a
    deep crevasse.
When we got him out one leg hung limp, and his
    brow was wreathed with pain,
And he says: "'Tis badly broken, boys, and I'll
    never walk again.
It's death for all if ye linger here, and that's no
    cursèd lie;
Go on, go on while the trail is good, and leave me
    down to die."
He raved and swore, but we tended him with our
    uncouth, clumsy care.
The camp-fire gleamed and he gazed and dreamed
    with a fixed and curious stare.
Then all at once he grabbed my gun and he put
    it to his head,
And he says: "I'll fix it for you, boys"—them are
    the words he said.

BALLAD OF THE NORTHERN LIGHTS

So we sewed him up in a canvas sack and we slung
    him to a tree;
And the stars like needles stabbed our eyes, and
    woeful men were we.
And on we went on our woeful way, wrapped in a
    daze of dream,
And the Northern Lights in the crystal nights
    came forth with a mystic gleam.
They danced and they danced the devil-dance over
    the naked snow;
And soft they rolled like a tide upshoaled with a
    ceaseless ebb and flow.
They rippled green with a wondrous sheen, they
    fluttered out like a fan;
They spread with a blaze of rose-pink rays never
    yet seen of man.
They writhed like a brood of angry snakes, hissing
    and sulphur pale;
Then swift they changed to a dragon vast, lashing
    a cloven tail.
It seemed to us, as we gazed aloft with an ever-
    lasting stare,
The sky was a pit of bale and dread, and a monster
    revelled there.

We climbed the rise of a hog-back range that was
    desolate and drear,
When the Sailor Swede had a crazy fit, and he got
    to talking queer.

BALLAD OF THE NORTHERN LIGHTS

He talked of his home in Oregon and the peach
    trees all in bloom,
And the fern head-high, and the topaz sky, and the
    forest's scented gloom.
He talked of the sins of his misspent life, and then
    he seemed to brood,
And I watched him there like a fox a hare, for I
    knew it was not good.
And sure enough in the dim dawn-light I missed
    him from the tent,
And a fresh trail broke through the crusted snow,
    and I knew not where it went.
But I followed it o'er the seamless waste, and I
    found him at shut of day,
Naked there as a new-born babe—so I left him
    where he lay.

Day after day was sinister, and I fought fierce-eyed
    despair,
And I clung to life, and I struggled on, I knew not
    why nor where.
I packed my grub in short relays, and I cowered
    down in my tent,
And the world around was purged of sound like a
    frozen continent.
Day after day was dark as death, but ever and
    ever at nights,
With a brilliancy that grew and grew, blazed up
    the Northern Lights.

BALLAD OF THE NORTHERN LIGHTS

They rolled around with a soundless sound like
    softly bruiséd silk;
They poured into the bowl of the sky with the
    gentle flow of milk.
In eager, pulsing violet their wheeling chariots
    came,
Or they poised above the Polar rim like a coronal
    of flame.
From depths of darkness fathomless their lancing
    rays were hurled,
Like the all-combining search-lights of the navies
    of the world.
There on the roof-pole of the world as one be-
    witched I gazed,
And howled and grovelled like a beast as the awful
    splendors blazed.
My eyes were seared, yet thralled I peered through
    the parka hood nigh blind;
But I staggered on to the lights that shone, and
    never I looked behind.

There is a mountain round and low that lies by
    the Polar rim,
And I climbed its height in a whirl of light, and I
    peered o'er its jaggéd brim;
And there in a crater deep and vast, ungained,
    unguessed of men,
The mystery of the Arctic world was flashed into
    my ken.

BALLAD OF THE NORTHERN LIGHTS

For there these poor dim eyes of mine beheld the
    sight of sights—
That hollow ring was the source and spring of the
    mystic Northern Lights.

Then I staked that place from crown to base, and
    I hit the homeward trail.
Ah, God! it was good, though my eyes were blurred,
    and I crawled like a sickly snail.
In that vast white world where the silent sky
    communes with the silent snow,
In hunger and cold and misery I wandered to and
    fro.
But the Lord took pity on my pain, and He led me
    to the sea,
And some ice-bound whalers heard my moan, and
    they fed and sheltered me.
They fed the feeble scarecrow thing that stumbled
    out of the wild
With the ravaged face of a mask of death and the
    wandering wits of a child—
A craven, cowering bag of bones that once had been
    a man.
They tended me and they brought me back to the
    world, and here I am.

Some say that the Northern Lights are the glare
    of the Arctic ice and snow;

BALLAD OF THE NORTHERN LIGHTS

And some that it's electricity, and nobody seems
to know.

But I'll tell you now—and if I lie, may my lips be
stricken dumb—

It's a *mine*, a mine of the precious stuff that men
call radium.

It's a million dollars a pound, they say, and there's
tons and tons in sight.

You can see it gleam in a golden stream in the
solitudes of night.

And it's mine, all mine—and say! if you have a
hundred plunks to spare,

I'll let you have the chance of your life, I'll sell
you a quarter share.

You turn it down?   Well, I'll make it ten, seeing
as you are my friend.

Nothing doing?   Say! don't be hard—have you
got a dollar to lend?

Just a dollar to help me out, I know you'll treat me
white;

I'll do as much for you some day . . . God
bless you, sir; good-night.

THE BALLAD OF THE BLACK FOX
SKIN

There was Claw-fingered Kitty and Windy Ike
    living the life of shame,
When unto them in the Long, Long Night came
    the man-who-had-no-name;
Bearing his prize of a black fox pelt, out of the Wild
    he came.

His cheeks were blanched as the flume-head foam
    when the brown spring freshets flow;
Deep in their dark, sin-calcined pits were his sombre
    eyes aglow;
They knew him far for the fitful man who spat
    forth blood on the snow.

"Did ever you see such a skin?" quoth he; "there's
    nought in the world so fine—
Such fullness of fur as black as the night, such
    lustre, such size, such shine;
It's life to a one-lunged man like me; it's London,
    it's women, it's wine.

29

BALLAD OF THE BLACK FOX SKIN

"The Moose-hides called it the devil-fox, and
    swore that no man could kill;
That he who hunted it, soon or late, must surely
    suffer some ill;
But I laughed at them and their old squaw-tales.
    Ha! Ha! I'm laughing still.

"For look ye, the skin—it's as smooth as sin, and
    black as the core of the Pit.
By gun or by trap, whatever the hap, I swore I
    would capture it;
By star and by star afield and afar, I hunted and
    would not quit.

"For the devil-fox, it was swift and sly, and it
    seemed to fleer at me;
I would wake in fright by the camp-fire light,
    hearing its evil glee;
Into my dream its eyes would gleam, and its
    shadow would I see.

"It sniffed and ran from the ptarmigan I had
    poisoned to excess;
Unharmed it sped from my wrathful lead ('twas
    as if I shot by guess);
Yet it came by night in the stark moonlight to
    mock at my weariness.

BALLAD OF THE BLACK FOX SKIN

"I tracked it up where the mountains hunch like
    the vertebrae of the world;
I tracked it down to the death-still pits where the
    avalanche is hurled;
From the glooms to the sacerdotal snows, where the
    carded clouds are curled.

"From the vastitudes where the world protrudes
    through clouds like seas up-shoaled,
I held its track till it led me back to the land I had
    left of old—
The land I had looted many moons. I was weary
    and sick and cold.

"I was sick, soul-sick, of the futile chase, and there
    and then I swore
The foul fiend fox might scathless go, for I would
    hunt no more;
Then I rubbed mine eyes in a vast surprise—it
    stood by my cabin door.

"A rifle raised in the wraith-like gloom, and a
    vengeful shot that sped;
A howl that would thrill a cream-faced corpse—
    and the demon fox lay dead. . . .
Yet there was never a sign of wound, and never a
    drop he bled.

BALLAD OF THE BLACK FOX SKIN

"So that was the end of the great black fox, and
      here is the prize I've won;
And now for a drink to cheer me up—I've mushed
      since the early sun;
We'll drink a toast to the sorry ghost of the fox
      whose race is run."

II.

Now Claw-fingered Kitty and Windy Ike, bad as
      the worst were they;
In their road-house down by the river-trail they
      waited and watched for prey;
With wine and song they joyed night long, and
      they slept like swine by day.

For things were done in the Midnight Sun that no
      tongue will ever tell;
And men there be who walk earth-free, but whose
      names are writ in hell—
Are writ in flames with the guilty names of Fournier
      and Labelle.

Put not your trust in a poke of dust would ye sleep
      the sleep of sin;
For there be those who would rob your clothes ere
      yet the dawn comes in;
And a prize likewise in a woman's eyes is a peerless
      black fox skin.

BALLAD OF THE BLACK FOX SKIN

Put your faith in the mountain cat if you lie within
his lair;
Trust the fangs of the mother-wolf, and the claws
of the lead-ripped bear;
But oh, of the wiles and the gold-tooth smiles of a
dance-hall wench beware!

Wherefore it was beyond all laws that lusts of man
restrain,
A man drank deep and sank to sleep never to wake
again;
And the Yukon swallowed through a hole the cold
corpse of the slain.

III.

The black fox skin a shadow cast from the roof nigh
to the floor;
And sleek it seemed and soft it gleamed, and the
woman stroked it o'er;
And the man stood by with a brooding eye, and
gnashed his teeth and swore.

When thieves and thugs fall out and fight there's
fell arrears to pay;
And soon or late sin meets its fate, and so it fell
one day
That Claw-fingered Kitty and Windy Ike fanged
up like dogs at bay.

BALLAD OF THE BLACK FOX SKIN

"The skin is mine, all mine," she cried; "I did the
deed alone."
"It's share and share with a guilt-yoked pair," he
hissed in a pregnant tone;
And so they snarled like malamutes over a mil-
dewed bone.

And so they fought, by fear untaught, till haply it
befell
One dawn of day she slipped away to Dawson town
to sell
The fruit of sin, this black fox skin that had made
their lives a hell.

She slipped away as still he lay, she clutched the
wondrous fur;
Her pulses beat, her foot was fleet, her fear was as
a spur;
She laughed with glee, she did not see him rise
and follow her.

The bluffs uprear and grimly peer far over Dawson
town;
They see its lights a blaze o' nights and harshly
they look down;
They mock the plan and plot of man with grim,
ironic frown.

BALLAD OF THE BLACK FOX SKIN

The trail was steep; 'twas at the time when swiftly
    sinks the snow;
All honey-combed, the river ice was rotting down
    below;
The river chafed beneath its rind with many a
    mighty throe.

And up the swift and oozy drift a woman climbed
    in fear,
Clutching to her a black fox fur as if she held it
    dear;
And hard she pressed it to her breast—then Windy
    Ike drew near.

She made no moan—her heart was stone—she read
    his smiling face,
And like a dream flashed all her life's dark horror
    and disgrace;
A moment only—with a snarl he hurled her into
    space.

She rolled for nigh an hundred feet; she bounded
    like a ball;
From crag to crag she carromed down through snow
    and timber fall; . . .
A hole gaped in the river ice; the spray flashed—
    that was all.

BALLAD OF THE BLACK FOX SKIN

A bird sang for the joy of spring, so piercing sweet
    and frail;
And blinding bright the land was dight in gay and
    glittering mail;
And with a wondrous black fox skin a man slid
    down the trail.

IV.

A wedge-faced man there was who ran along the
    river bank,
Who stumbled through each drift and slough, and
    ever slipped and sank,
And ever cursed his Maker's name, and ever
    "hooch" he drank.

He travelled like a hunted thing, hard harried, sore
    distrest;
The old grandmother moon crept out from her
    cloud-quilted nest;
The aged mountains mocked at him in their prim-
    eval rest.

Grim shadows diapered the snow; the air was
    strangely mild;
The valley's girth was dumb with mirth, the
    laughter of the wild;
The still, sardonic laughter of an ogre o'er a child.

BALLAD OF THE BLACK FOX SKIN

The river writhed beneath the ice; it groaned like
    one in pain,
And yawning chasms opened wide, and closed and
    yawned again;
And sheets of silver heaved on high until they split
    in twain

From out the road-house by the trail they saw a
    man afar
Make for the narrow river-reach where the swift
    cross-currents are;
Where, frail and worn, the ice is torn and the angry
    waters jar.

But they did not see him crash and sink into the
    icy flow;
They did not see him clinging there, gripped by
    the undertow,
Clawing with bleeding finger-nails at the jagged
    ice and snow.

They found a note beside the hole where he had
    stumbled in:
"Here met his fate by evil luck a man who lived
    in sin,
And to the one who loves me least I leave this
    black fox skin."

37

BALLAD OF THE BLACK FOX SKIN

And strange it is; for, though they searched the
river all around,
No trace or sign of black fox skin was ever after
found;
Though one man said he saw the tread of *hoofs*
deep in the ground.

THE BALLAD OF PIOUS PETE

"The North has got him."—Yukonism.

I tried to refine that neighbor of mine, honest to
    God, I did.
I grieved for his fate, and early and late I watched
    over him like a kid.
I gave him excuse, I bore his abuse in every way
    that I could;
I swore to prevail; I camped on his trail; I plotted
    and planned for his good.
By day and by night I strove in men's sight to
    gather him into the fold,
With precept and prayer, with hope and despair, in
    hunger and hardship and cold.
I followed him into Gehennas of sin, I sat where
    the sirens sit;
In the shade of the Pole, for the sake of his soul, I
    strove with the powers of the Pit.
I shadowed him down to the scrofulous town; I
    dragged him from dissolute brawls;
But I killed the galoot when he started to shoot
    electricity into my walls.

THE BALLAD OF PIOUS PETE

God knows what I did he should seek to be rid of
    one who would save him from shame.
God knows what I bore that night when he swore
    and bade me make tracks from his claim.
I started to tell of the horrors of hell, when sudden
    his eyes lit like coals;
And "Chuck it," says he, "don't persecute me with
    your cant and your saving of souls."
I'll swear I was mild as I'd be with a child, but he
    called me the son of a slut;
And, grabbing his gun with a leap and a run, he
    threatened my face with the butt.
So what could I do (I leave it to you)? With curses
    he harried me forth;
Then he was alone, and I was alone, and over us
    menaced the North.

Our cabins were near; I could see, I could hear;
    but between us there rippled the creek;
And all summer through, with a rancor that grew,
    he would pass me and never would speak.
Then a shuddery breath like the coming of Death
    crept down from the peaks far away;
The water was still; the twilight was chill; the sky
    was a tatter of gray.
Swift came the Big Cold, and opal and gold the
    lights of the witches arose;

THE BALLAD OF PIOUS PETE

The frost-tyrant clinched, and the valley was
    cinched by the stark and cadaverous snows.
The trees were like lace where the star-beams
    could chase, each leaf was a jewel agleam.
The soft white hush lapped the Northland and
    wrapped us round in a crystalline dream;
So still I could hear quite loud in my ear the swish
    of the pinions of time;
So bright I could see, as plain as could be, the wings
    of God's angels ashine.

As I read in the Book I would oftentimes look to
    that cabin just over the creek.
Ah me, it was sad and evil and bad, two neighbors
    who never would speak!
I knew that full well like a devil in hell he was
    hatching out, early and late,
A system to bear through the frost-spangled air
    the warm, crimson waves of his hate.
I only could peer and shudder and fear—'twas
    ever so ghastly and still;
But I knew over there in his lonely despair he was
    plotting me terrible ill.
I knew that he nursed a malice accurst, like the
    blast of a winnowing flame;
I pleaded aloud for a shield, for a shroud—Oh,
    God! then calamity came.

THE BALLAD OF PIOUS PETE

Mad! If I'm mad then you too are mad; but it's
all in the point of view.
If you'd looked at them things gallivantin' on
wings, all purple and green and blue;
If you'd noticed them twist, as they mounted and
hissed like scorpions dim in the dark;
If you'd seen them rebound with a horrible sound,
and spitefully spitting a spark;
If you'd watched *It* with dread, as it hissed by your
bed, that thing with the feelers that crawls—
You'd have settled the brute that attempted to
shoot electricity into your walls.

Oh, some they were blue, and they slithered right
through; they were silent and squashy and
round;
And some they were green; they were wriggly and
lean; they writhed with so hateful a sound.
My blood seemed to freeze; I fell on my knees;
my face was a white splash of dread.
Oh, the Green and the Blue, they were gruesome to
view; but the worst of them all were the Red.
They came through the door, they came through
the floor, they came through the moss-
creviced logs.
They were savage and dire; they were whiskered
with fire; they bickered like malamute dogs.

THE BALLAD OF PIOUS PETE

They ravined in rings like iniquitous things; they
    gulped down the Green and the Blue.
I crinkled with fear whene'er they drew near, and
    nearer and nearer they drew.

And then came the crown of Horror's grim crown,
    the monster so loathsomely red.
Each eye was a pin that shot out and in, as, squid-
    like, it oozed to my bed;
So softly it crept with feelers that swept and quiv-
    ered like fine copper wire;
Its belly was white with a sulphurous light, its
    jaws were a-drooling with fire.
It came and it came; I could breathe of its flame,
    but never a wink could I look.
I thrust in its maw the Fount of the Law; I fended
    it off with the Book.
I was weak—oh, so weak—but I thrilled at its
    shriek, as wildly it fled in the night;
And deathlike I lay till the dawn of the day. (Was
    ever so welcome the light?)

I loaded my gun at the rise of the sun; to his cabin
    so softly I slunk.
My neighbor was there in the frost-freighted air,
    all wrapped in a robe in his bunk.

THE BALLAD OF PIOUS PETE

It muffled his moans; it outlined his bones, as
    feebly he twisted about;
His gums were so black, and his lips seemed to
    crack, and his teeth all were loosening out.
'Twas a death's head that peered through the
    tangle of beard; 'twas a face I will never
    forget;
Sunk eyes full of woe, and they troubled me so
    with their pleadings and anguish, and yet
As I rested my gaze in a misty amaze on the
    scurvy-degenerate wreck,
I thought of the Things with the dragon-fly wings,
    then laid I my gun on his neck.
He gave out a cry that was faint as a sigh, like a
    perishing malamute,
And he says unto me, "I'm converted," says he;
    "for Christ's sake, Peter, don't shoot!"

       *   *   *   *   *   *

They're taking me out with an escort about, and
    under a sergeant's care;
I am humbled indeed, for I'm 'cuffed to a Swede
    that thinks he's a millionaire.
But it's all Gospel true what I'm telling to you—
    up there where the Shadow falls—
That I settled Sam Noot when he started to shoot
    electricity into my walls.

THE BALLAD OF BLASPHEMOUS BILL

I took a contract to bury the body of blasphemous
    Bill MacKie,
Whenever, wherever or whatsoever the manner of
    death he die—
Whether he die in the light o' day or under the
    peak-faced moon;
In cabin or dance-hall, camp or dive, mucklucks
    or patent shoon;
On velvet tundra or virgin peak, by glacier, drift
    or draw;
In muskeg hollow or canyon gloom, by avalanche,
    fang or claw;
By battle, murder or sudden wealth, by pestilence,
    hooch or lead—
I swore on the Book I would follow and look till I
    found my tombless dead.

For Bill was a dainty kind of cuss, and his mind
    was mighty sot
On a dinky patch with flowers and grass in a civil-
    ized bone-yard lot.

BALLAD OF BLASPHEMOUS BILL

And where he died or how he died, it didn't matter
a damn
So long as he had a grave with frills and a tomb-
stone "epigram."
So I promised him, and he paid the price in good
cheechako coin
(Which the same I blowed in that very night down
in the Tenderloin).
Then I painted a three-foot slab of pine: "Here
lies poor Bill MacKie,"
And I hung it up on my cabin wall and I waited
for Bill to die.

Years passed away, and at last one day came a
squaw with a story strange,
Of a long-deserted line of traps 'way back of the
Bighorn range;
Of a little hut by the great divide, and a white man
stiff and still,
Lying there by his lonesome self, and I figured it
must be Bill.
So I thought of the contract I'd made with him,
and I took down from the shelf
The swell black box with the silver plate he'd picked
out for hisself;
And I packed it full of grub and "hooch," and I
slung it on the sleigh;
Then I harnessed up my team of dogs and was off
at dawn of day.

BALLAD OF BLASPHEMOUS BILL

You know what it's like in the Yukon wild when
  it's sixty-nine below;
When the ice-worms wriggle their purple heads
  through the crust of the pale blue snow;
When the pine-trees crack like little guns in the
  silence of the wood,
And the icicles hang down like tusks under the
  parka hood;
When the stove-pipe smoke breaks sudden off, and
  the sky is weirdly lit,
And the careless feel of a bit of steel burns like a
  red-hot spit;
When the mercury is a frozen ball, and the frost-
  fiend stalks to kill—
Well, it was just like that that day when I set out
  to look for Bill.

Oh, the awful hush that seemed to crush me down
  on every hand,
As I blundered blind with a trail to find through
  that blank and bitter land;
Half dazed, half crazed in the winter wild, with its
  grim heart-breaking woes,
And the ruthless strife for a grip on life that only
  the sourdough knows!
North by the compass, North I pressed; river and
  peak and plain
Passed like a dream I slept to lose and I waked to
  dream again

BALLAD OF BLASPHEMOUS BILL

River and plain and mighty peak—and who could
    stand unawed?
As their summits blazed, he could stand undazed
    at the foot of the throne of God.
North, aye, North, through a land accurst, shunned
    by the scouring brutes,
And all I heard was my own harsh word and the
    whine of the malamutes,
Till at last I came to a cabin squat, built in the side
    of a hill,
And I burst in the door, and there on the floor,
    frozen to death, lay Bill.

Ice, white ice, like a winding-sheet, sheathing each
    smoke-grimed wall;
Ice on the stove-pipe, ice on the bed, ice gleaming
    over all;
Sparkling ice on the dead man's chest, glittering
    ice in his hair,
Ice on his fingers, ice in his heart, ice in his glassy
    stare;
Hard as a log and trussed like a frog, with his arms
    and legs outspread.
I gazed at the coffin I'd brought for him, and I
    gazed at the gruesome dead,
And at last I spoke: "Bill liked his joke; but still,
    goldarn his eyes,
A man had ought to consider his mates in the way
    he goes and dies."

BALLAD OF BLASPHEMOUS BILL

Have you ever stood in an Arctic hut in the shadow
      of the Pole,
With a little coffin six by three and a grief you
      can't control?
Have you ever sat by a frozen corpse that looks
      at you with a grin,
And that seems to say: "You may try all day, but
      you'll never jam me in?"
I'm not a man of the quitting kind, but I never
      felt so blue
As I sat there gazing at that stiff and studying
      what I'd do.
Then I rose and I kicked off the husky dogs that
      were nosing round about,
And I lit a roaring fire in the stove, and I started
      to thaw Bill out.

Well, I thawed and thawed for thirteen days, but
      it didn't seem no good;
His arms and legs stuck out like pegs, as if they
      was made of wood.
Till at last I said: "It ain't no use—he's froze too
      hard to thaw;
He's obstinate, and he won't lie straight, so I guess
      I got to—*saw*."
So I sawed off poor Bill's arms and legs, and I laid
      him snug and straight
In the little coffin he picked hisself, with the dinky
      silver plate;

BALLAD OF BLASPHEMOUS BILL

And I came nigh near to shedding a tear as I nailed
    him safely down;
Then I stowed him away in my Yukon sleigh, and
    I started back to town.

So I buried him as the contract was in a narrow
    grave and deep,
And there he's waiting the Great Clean-up, when
    the Judgment sluice-heads sweep;
And I smoke my pipe and I meditate in the light of
    the Midnight Sun,
And sometimes I wonder if they *was*, the awful
    things I done.
And as I sit and the parson talks, expounding of
    the Law,
I often think of poor old Bill—*and how hard he was
    to saw.*

THE BALLAD OF ONE-EYED MIKE

This is the tale that was told to me by the man with
the crystal eye,
As I smoked my pipe in the camp-fire light, and the
Glories swept the sky;
As the Northlights gleamed and curved and streamed,
and the bottle of "hooch" was dry.

A man once aimed that my life be shamed, and
wrought me a deathly wrong;
I vowed one day I would well repay, but the heft
of his hate was strong.
He thonged me East and he thonged me West; he
harried me back and forth,
Till I fled in fright from his peerless spite to the
bleak, bald-headed North.

And there I lay, and for many a day I hatched plan
after plan,
For a golden haul of the wherewithal to crush and
to kill my man;

THE BALLAD OF ONE-EYED MIKE

And there I strove, and there I clove through the
    drift of icy streams;
And there I fought, and there I sought for the pay
    streak of my dreams.

So twenty years, with their hopes and fears and
    smiles and tears and such,
Went by and left me long bereft of hope of the
    Midas touch;
About as fat as a chancel rat, and lo! despite my
    will,
In the weary fight I had clean lost sight of the man
    I sought to kill.

'Twas so far away, that evil day when I prayed
    the Prince of Gloom
For the savage strength and the sullen length of
    life to work his doom.
Nor sign nor word had I seen or heard, and it
    happed so long ago;
My youth was gone and my memory wan, and I
    willed it even so.

It fell one night in the waning light by the Yukon's
    oily flow,
I smoked and sat as I marvelled at the sky's port-
    winey glow;

Till it paled away to an absinthe gray, and the
    river seemed to shrink,
All wobbly flakes and wriggling snakes and goblin
    eyes a-wink.

'Twas weird to see and it 'wildered me in a queer,
    hypnotic dream,
Till I saw a spot like an inky blot come floating
    down the stream;
It bobbed and swung; it sheered and hung; it
    romped round in a ring;
It seemed to play in a tricksome way; it sure was
    a merry thing.

In freakish flights strange oily lights came fluttering
    round its head,
Like butterflies of a monster size—then I knew it
    for the Dead.
Its face was rubbed and slicked and scrubbed as
    smooth as a shaven pate;
In the silver snakes that the water makes it gleamed
    like a dinner-plate.

It gurgled near, and clear and clear and large and
    large it grew;
It stood upright in a ring of light and it looked me
    through and through.

THE BALLAD OF ONE-EYED MIKE

It weltered round with a woozy sound, and ere I
    could retreat,
With the witless roll of a sodden soul it wantoned
    to my feet.

And here I swear by this Cross I wear, I heard that
    "floater" say:
"I am the man from whom you ran, the man you
    sought to slay.
That you may note and gaze and gloat, and say
    'Revenge is sweet,'
In the grit and grime of the river's slime I am
    rotting at your feet.

"The ill we rue we must e'en undo, though it rive
    us bone from bone;
So it came about that I sought you out, for I prayed
    I might atone.
I did you wrong, and for long and long I sought
    where you might live;
And now you're found, though I'm dead and
    drowned, I beg you to forgive."

So sad it seemed, and its cheek-bones gleamed,
    and its fingers flicked the shore;
And it lapped and lay in a weary way, and its hands
    met to implore;

THE BALLAD OF ONE-EYED MIKE

That I gently said: "Poor, restless dead, I would
    never work you woe;
Though the wrong you rue you can ne'er undo,
    I forgave you long ago."

Then, wonder-wise, I rubbed my eyes and I woke
    from a horrid dream.
The moon rode high in the naked sky, and some-
    thing bobbed in the stream.
It held my sight in a patch of light, and then it
    sheered from the shore;
It dipped and sank by a hollow bank, and I never
    saw it more.

This was the tale he told to me, that man so warped
    and gray,
Ere he slept and dreamed, and the camp-fire gleamed
    in his eye in a wolfish way—
That crystal eye that raked the sky in the weird
    Auroral ray.

THE BALLAD OF THE BRAND

'Twas up in a land long famed for gold, where
    women were far and rare,
Tellus, the smith, had taken to wife a maiden
    amazingly fair;
Tellus, the brawny worker in iron, hairy and heavy
    of hand,
Saw her and loved her and bore her away from the
    tribe of a Southern land;
Deeming her worthy to queen his home and mother
    him little ones,
That the name of Tellus, the master smith, might
    live in his stalwart sons.

Now there was little of law in the land, and evil
    doings were rife,
And every man who joyed in his home guarded the
    fame of his wife;
For there were those of the silver tongue and the
    honeyed art to beguile,
Who would cozen the heart from a woman's breast
    and damn her soul with a smile.

56

THE BALLAD OF THE BRAND

And there were women too quick to heed a look
 or a whispered word,
And once in a while a man was slain, and the ire
 of the King was stirred;
So far and wide he proclaimed his wrath, and this
 was the law he willed:
"That whosoever killeth a man, even shall he be
 killed."

Now Tellus, the smith, he trusted his wife; his
 heart was empty of fear.
High on the hill was the gleam of their hearth, a
 beacon of love and cheer.
High on the hill they builded their bower, where
 the broom and the bracken meet;
Under a grave of oaks it was, hushed and drowsily
 sweet.
Here he enshrined her, his dearest saint, his idol,
 the light of his eye;
Her kisses rested upon his lips as brushes a butterfly.
The weight of her arms around his neck was light
 as the thistle down;
And sweetly she studied to win his smile, and gently
 she mocked his frown.
And when at the close of the dusty day his clang-
 orous toil was done,
She hastened to meet him down the way all lit by
 the amber sun.

57

THE BALLAD OF THE BRAND

Their dove-cot gleamed in the golden light, a
temple of stainless love;
Like the hanging cup of a big blue flower was the
topaz sky above.
The roses and lilies yearned to her, as swift through
their throng she pressed;
A little white, fragile, fluttering thing that lay like
a child on his breast.
Then the heart of Tellus, the smith, was proud, and
sang for the joy of life,
And there in the bronzing summertide he thanked
the gods for his wife.

Now there was one called Philo, a scribe, a man of
exquisite grace,
Carved like the god Apollo in limb, fair as Adonis
in face;
Eager and winning of manner, full of such radiant
charm,
Womenkind fought for his favor and loved to their
uttermost harm.
Such was his craft and his knowledge, such was his
skill at the game,
Never was woman could flout him, so be he plotted
her shame.
And so he drank deep of pleasure, and then it fell
on a day
He gazed on the wife of Tellus and marked her
out for his prey.

THE BALLAD OF THE BRAND

Tellus, the smith, was merry, and the time of the
     year it was June,
So he said to his stalwart helpers: "Shut down
     the forge at noon.
Go ye and joy in the sunshine, rest in the coolth of
     the grove,
Drift on the dreamy river, every man with his love."
Then to himself: "Oh, Beloved, sweet will be your
     surprise;
To-day will we sport like children, laugh in each
     other's eyes;
Weave gay garlands of poppies, crown each other
     with flowers,
Pull plump carp from the lilies, rifle the ferny
     bowers.
To-day with feasting and gladness the wine of
     Cyprus will flow;
To-day is the day we were wedded only a twelve-
     month ago."

The larks trilled high in the heavens; his heart was
     lyric with joy;
He plucked a posy of lilies; he sped like a love-sick
     boy.
He stole up the velvety pathway—his cottage was
     sunsteeped and still;
Vines honeysuckled the window; softly he peeped
     o'er the sill.

THE BALLAD OF THE BRAND

The lilies dropped from his fingers; devils were
    choking his breath;
Rigid with horror, he stiffened; ghastly his face
    was as death.
Like a nun whose faith in the Virgin is met with
    a prurient jibe,
He shrank—'twas the wife of his bosom in the
    arms of Philo, the scribe.

Tellus went back to his smithy; he reeled like a
    drunken man;
His heart was riven with anguish; his brain was
    brooding a plan.
Straight to his anvil he hurried; started his furnace
    aglow;
Heated his iron and shaped it with savage and
    masterful blow.
Sparks showered over and round him; swiftly under
    his hand
There at last it was finished—a hideous and in-
    famous Brand.

That night the wife of his bosom, the light of joy
    in her eyes,
Kissed him with words of rapture; but he knew
    that her words were lies.
Never was she so beguiling, never so merry of
    speech

THE BALLAD OF THE BRAND

(For passion ripens a woman as the sunshine
    ripens a peach).
He clenched his teeth into silence; he yielded up
    to her lure,
Though he knew that her breasts were heaving
    from the fire of her paramour.
"To-morrow," he said, "to-morrow"—he wove
    her hair in a strand,
Twisted it round his fingers and smiled as he
    thought of the Brand.

The morrow was come, and Tellus swiftly stole up
    the hill.
Butterflies drowsed in the noon-heat; coverts were
    sunsteeped and still.
Softly he padded the pathway unto the porch, and
    within
Heard he the low laugh of dalliance, heard he the
    rapture of sin.
Knew he her eyes were mystic with light that no
    man should see,
No man kindle and joy in, no man on earth save
    he.
And never for him would it kindle. The blood-
    lust surged in his brain;
Through the senseless stone could he see them,
    wanton and warily fain.

THE BALLAD OF THE BRAND

Horrible! Heaven he sought for, gained it and
    gloried and fell—
Oh, it was sudden—headlong into the nether-
    most hell. . . .

Was this he, Tellus, this marble? Tellus . . .
    not dreaming a dream?
Ah! sharp-edged as a javelin, was that a woman's
    scream?
Was it a door that shattered, shell-like, under his
    blow?
Was it his saint, that strumpet, dishevelled and
    cowering low?
Was it her lover, that wild thing, that twisted and
    gouged and tore?
Was it a man he was crushing, whose head he beat
    on the floor?
Laughing the while at its weakness, till sudden
    he stayed his hand—
Through the red ring of his madness flamed the
    thought of the Brand.

Then bound he the naked Philo with thongs that
    cut in the flesh,
And the wife of his bosom, fear-frantic, he gagged
    with a silken mesh,

62

THE BALLAD OF THE BRAND

Choking her screams into silence; bound her down
    by the hair;
Dragged her lover unto her under her frenzied
    stare.
In the heat of the hearth-fire embers he heated the
    hideous Brand;
Twisting her fingers open, he forced its haft in her
    hand.
He pressed it downward and downward; she felt
    the living flesh sear;
She saw the throe of her lover; she heard the scream
    of his fear.
Once, twice and thrice he forced her, heedless of
    prayer and shriek—
Once on the forehead of Philo, twice in the soft of
    his cheek.
Then (for the thing was finished) he said to the
    woman: "See
How you have branded your lover! Now will I
    let him go free."
He severed the thongs that bound him, laughing:
    "Revenge is sweet,"
And Philo, sobbing in anguish, feebly rose to his
    feet.
The man who was fair as Apollo, god-like in
    woman's sight,
Hideous now as a satyr, fled to the pity of night.

THE BALLAD OF THE BRAND

*Then came they before the Judgment Seat, and thus
spoke the Lord of the Land:*
*"He who seeketh his neighbor's wife shall suffer the
doom of the Brand.*
*Brutish and bold on his brow be it stamped, deep in
his cheek let it sear,*
*That every man may look on his shame, and shudder
and sicken and fear.*
*He shall hear their mock in the market-place, their
fleering jibe at the feast;*
*He shall seek the caves and the shroud of night, and
the fellowship of the beast.*
*Outcast forever from homes of men, far and far shall
he roam.*
*Such be the doom, sadder than death, of him who
shameth a home."*

THE BALLAD OF HARD-LUCK
HENRY

Now wouldn't you expect to find a man an awful
    crank
That's staked out nigh three hundred claims, and
    every one a blank;
That's followed every fool stampede, and seen the
    rise and fall
Of camps where men got gold in chunks and he got
    none at all;
That's prospected a bit of ground and sold it for
    a song
To see it yield a fortune to some fool that came
    along;
That's sunk a dozen bed-rock holes, and not a speck
    in sight,
Yet sees them take a million from the claims to
    left and right?
Now aren't things like that enough to drive a man
    to booze?
But Hard-Luck Smith was hoodoo-proof—he knew
    the way to lose.

BALLAD OF HARD-LUCK HENRY

'Twas in the fall of nineteen four—leap-year I've
    heard them say—
When Hard-Luck came to Hunker Creek and took
    a hillside lay.
And lo! as if to make amends for all the futile
    past,
Late in the year he struck it rich, the real pay-
    streak at last.
The riffles of his sluicing-box were choked with
    speckled earth,
And night and day he worked that lay for all that
    he was worth.
And when in chill December's gloom his lucky
    lease expired,
He found that he had made a stake as big as he
    desired.

One day while meditating on the waywardness of
    fate,
He felt the ache of lonely man to find a fitting mate;
A petticoated pard to cheer his solitary life,
A woman with soft, soothing ways, a confidant, a
    wife.
And while he cooked his supper on his little Yukon
    stove,
He wished that he had staked a claim in Love's
    rich treasure-trove;

BALLAD OF HARD-LUCK HENRY

When suddenly he paused and held aloft a Yukon
      egg,
For there in pencilled letters was the magic name
      of Peg.

You know these Yukon eggs of ours—some pink,
      some green, some blue—
A dollar per, assorted tints, assorted flavors too.
The supercilious cheechako might designate them
      high,
But one acquires a taste for them and likes them
      by-and-by.
Well, Hard-Luck Henry took this egg and held it
      to the light,
And there was more faint pencilling that sorely
      taxed his sight.
At last he made it out, and then the legend ran like
      this—
"Will Klondike miner write to Peg, Plumhollow,
      Squashville, Wis.?"

That night he got to thinking of this far-off, un-
      known fair;
It seemed so sort of opportune, an answer to his
      prayer.

BALLAD OF HARD-LUCK HENRY

She flitted sweetly through his dreams, she haunted
    him by day,
She smiled through clouds of nicotine, she cheered
    his weary way.
At last he yielded to the spell; his course of love
    he set—
Wisconsin his objective point; his object, Margaret.

With every mile of sea and land his longing grew
    and grew.
He practised all his pretty words, and these, I fear,
    were few.
At last, one frosty evening, with a cold chill down
    his spine,
He found himself before her house, the threshold
    of the shrine.
His courage flickered to a spark, then glowed with
    sudden flame—
He knocked; he heard a welcome word; she came
    —his goddess came.
Oh, she was fair as any flower, and huskily he spoke:
"I'm all the way from Klondike, with a mighty
    heavy poke.
I'm looking for a lassie, one whose Christian name
    is Peg,
Who sought a Klondike miner, and who wrote it
    on an egg."

BALLAD OF HARD-LUCK HENRY

The lassie gazed at him a space, her cheeks grew
    rosy red;
She gazed at him with tear-bright eyes, then ten-
    derly she said:
"Yes, lonely Klondike miner, it is true my name is
    Peg.
It's also true I longed for you and wrote it on an
    egg.
My heart went out to someone in that land of night
    and cold;
But oh, I fear that Yukon egg must have been
    mighty old.
I waited long, I hoped and feared; you should have
    come before;
I've been a wedded woman now for eighteen months
    or more.
I'm sorry, since you've come so far, you ain't the
    one that wins;
But won't you take a step inside—*I'll let you see
the twins.*"

THE MAN FROM ELDORADO

He's the man from Eldorado, and he's just arrived
      in town,
  In moccasins and oily buckskin shirt.
He's gaunt as any Indian, and pretty nigh as brown;
  He's greasy, and he smells of sweat and dirt.
He sports a crop of whiskers that would shame a
      healthy hog;
  Hard work has racked his joints and stooped
      his back;
He slops along the sidewalk followed by his yellow
      dog,
  But he's got a bunch of gold-dust in his sack.

He seems a little wistful as he blinks at all the
      lights,
  And maybe he is thinking of his claim
And the dark and dwarfish cabin where he lay and
      dreamed at nights,
  (Thank God, he'll never see the place again!)

70

THE MAN FROM ELDORADO

Where he lived on tinned tomatoes, beef embalmed
    and sourdough bread,
  On rusty beans and bacon furred with mould;
His stomach's out of kilter and his system full of
    lead,
  But it's over, and his poke is full of gold.

He has panted at the windlass, he has loaded in the
    drift,
  He has pounded at the face of oozy clay;
He has taxed himself to sickness, dark and damp
    and double shift,
  He has labored like a demon night and day.
And now, praise God, it's over, and he seems to
    breathe again
  Of new-mown hay, the warm, wet, friendly loam;
He sees a snowy orchard in a green and dimpling
    plain,
  And a little vine-clad cottage, and it's—Home.

II.

He's the man from Eldorado, and he's had a bite
    and sup,
  And he's met in with a drouthy friend or two;
He's cached away his gold-dust, but he's sort of
    bucking up,
  So he's kept enough to-night to see him through.

THE MAN FROM ELDORADO

His eye is bright and genial, his tongue no longer
    lags;
  His heart is brimming o'er with joy and mirth;
He may be far from savory, he may be clad in rags,
  But to-night he feels as if he owns the earth.

Says he: "Boys, here is where the shaggy North
    and I will shake;
  I thought I'd never manage to get free.
I kept on making misses; but at last I've got my
    stake;
  There's no more thawing frozen muck for me.
I am going to God's Country, where I'll live the
    simple life;
  I'll buy a bit of land and make a start;
I'll carve a little homestead, and I'll win a little
    wife,
  And raise ten little kids to cheer my heart."

They signified their sympathy by crowding to the
    bar;
  They bellied up three deep and drank his health.
He shed a radiant smile around and smoked a rank
    cigar;
  They wished him honor, happiness and wealth.
They drank unto his wife to be—that unsuspecting
    maid;
  They drank unto his children half a score;

THE MAN FROM ELDORADO

And when they got through drinking very ten-
derly they laid
The man from Eldorado on the floor.

III.

He's the man from Eldorado, and he's only start-
ing in
To cultivate a thousand-dollar jag.
His poke is full of gold-dust and his heart is full of
sin,
And he's dancing with a girl called Muckluck Mag.
She's as light as any fairy; she's as pretty as a peach;
She's mistress of the witchcraft to beguile;
There's sunshine in her manner, there is music in
her speech,
And there's concentrated honey in her smile.

Oh, the fever of the dance-hall and the glitter and
the shine,
The beauty, and the jewels, and the whirl,
The madness of the music, the rapture of the wine,
The languorous allurement of a girl!
She is like a lost madonna; he is gaunt, unkempt
and grim;
But she fondles him and gazes in his eyes;
Her kisses seek his heavy lips, and soon it seems
to him
He has staked a little claim in Paradise.

THE MAN FROM ELDORADO

'Who's for a juicy two-step?" cries the master of
    the floor;
  The music throbs with soft, seductive beat.
There's glitter, gilt and gladness; there are pretty
    girls galore;
  There's a woolly man with moccasins on feet.
They know they've got him going; he is buying
    wine for all;
  They crowd around as buzzards at a feast,
Then when his poke is empty they boost him from
    the hall,
  And spurn him in the gutter like a beast.

He's the man from Eldorado, and he's painting
    red the town;
  Behind he leaves a trail of yellow dust;
In a whirl of senseless riot he is ramping up and
    down;
  There's nothing checks his madness and his
    lust.
And soon the word is passed around—it travels
    like a flame;
  They fight to clutch his hand and call him friend,
The chevaliers of lost repute, the dames of sorry
    fame;
  Then comes the grim awakening—the end.

THE MAN FROM ELDORADO

IV.

He's the man from Eldorado, and he gives a grand
affair;
There's feasting, dancing, wine without re-
straint.
The smooth Beau Brummels of the bar, the faro
men, are there;
The tinhorns and purveyors of red paint;
The sleek and painted women, their predacious
eyes aglow—
Sure Klondike City never saw the like;
Then Muckluck Mag proposed the toast, "The giver
of the show,
The livest sport that ever hit the pike."

The "live one" rises to his feet; he stammers to
reply—
And then there comes before his muddled brain
A vision of green vastitudes beneath an April
sky,
And clover pastures drenched with silver rain.
He knows that it can never be, that he is down and
out;
Life leers at him with foul and fetid breath;
And then amid the revelry, the song and cheer and
shout,
He suddenly grows grim and cold as death.

THE MAN FROM ELDORADO

He grips the table tensely, and he says: "Dear
    friends of mine,
  I've let you dip your fingers in my purse;
I've crammed you at my table, and I've drowned
    you in my wine,
  And I've little left to give you but—my curse.
I've failed supremely in my plans; it's rather late
    to whine;
  My poke is mighty weasened up and small.
I thank you each for coming here; the happiness
    is mine—
  And now, you thieves and harlots, take it all."

He twists the thong from off his poke; he swings
    it o'er his head;
  The nuggets fall around their feet like grain.
They rattle over roof and wall; they scatter, roll
    and spread;
  The dust is like a shower of golden rain.
The guests a moment stand aghast, then grovel on
    the floor;
  They fight, and snarl, and claw, like beasts of
      prey;
And then, as everybody grabbed and everybody
    swore,
  The man from Eldorado slipped away.

THE MAN FROM ELDORADO

v.

He's the man from Eldorado, and they found him
    stiff and dead,
  Half covered by the freezing ooze and dirt.
A clotted Colt was in his hand, a hole was in his
    head,
  And he wore an old and oily buckskin shirt.
His eyes were fixed and horrible, as one who hails
    the end;
  The frost had set him rigid as a log;
And there, half lying on his breast, his last and only
    friend,
  There crouched and whined a mangy yellow dog.

MY FRIENDS

The man above was a murderer, the man below
    was a thief;
And I lay there in the bunk between, ailing beyond
    belief;
A weary armful of skin and bone, wasted with pain
    and grief.

My feet were froze, and the lifeless toes were purple
    and green and gray;
The little flesh that clung to my bones, you could
    punch it in holes like clay;
The skin on my gums was a sullen black, and slowly
    peeling away.

I was sure enough in a direful fix, and often I won-
    dered why
They did not take the chance that was left and
    leave me alone to die,
Or finish me off with a dose of dope—so utterly
    lost was I.

MY FRIENDS

But no; they brewed me the green-spruce tea, and
    nursed me there like a child;
And the homicide he was good to me, and bathed
    my sores and smiled;
And the thief he starved that I might be fed, and
    his eyes were kind and mild.

Yet they were woefully wicked men, and often at
    night in pain
I heard the murderer speak of his deed and dream
    it over again;
I heard the poor thief sorrowing for the dead self
    he had slain.

I'll never forget that bitter dawn, so evil, askew
    and gray,
When they wrapped me round in the skins of
    beasts and they bore me to a sleigh,
And we started out with the nearest post an hun-
    dred miles away.

I'll never forget the trail they broke, with its tense,
    unuttered woe;
And the crunch, crunch, crunch as their snow-
    shoes sank through the crust of the hollow
    snow;
And my breath would fail, and every beat of my
    heart was like a blow.

79

MY FRIENDS

And oftentimes I would die the death, yet wake
    up to life anew;
The sun would be all ablaze on the waste, and the
    sky a blighting blue,
And the tears would rise in my snow-blind eyes
    and furrow my cheeks like dew.

And the camps we made when their strength out-
    played and the day was pinched and wan;
And oh, the joy of that blessed halt, and how I
    did dread the dawn;
And how I hated the weary men who rose and
    dragged me on.

And oh, how I begged to rest, to rest—the snow
    was so sweet a shroud;
And oh, how I cried when they urged me on, cried
    and cursed them aloud;
Yet on they strained, all racked and pained, and
    sorely their backs were bowed.

And then it was all like a lurid dream, and I prayed
    for a swift release
From the ruthless ones who would not leave me to
    die alone in peace;
Till I wakened up and I found myself at the post
    of the Mounted Police.

MY FRIENDS

And there was my friend the murderer, and there
    was my friend the thief,
With bracelets of steel around their wrists, and
    wicked beyond belief:
But when they come to God's judgment seat—
    may I be allowed the brief.

THE PROSPECTOR

I strolled up old Bonanza, where I staked in ninety-
    eight,
  A-purpose to revisit the old claim.
I kept thinking mighty sadly of the funny ways of
    Fate,
  And the lads who once were with me in the
    game.
Poor boys, they're down-and-outers, and there's
    scarcely one to-day
  Can show a dozen colors in his poke;
And me, I'm still prospecting, old and battered,
    gaunt and gray,
  And I'm looking for a grub-stake, and I'm
    broke.

I strolled up old Bonanza. The same old moon
    looked down;
  The same old landmarks seemed to yearn to me;
But the cabins all were silent, and the flat, once like
    a town,
  Was mighty still and lonesome-like to see.

THE PROSPECTOR

There were piles and piles of tailings where we
    toiled with pick and pan,
  And turning round a bend I heard a roar,
And there a giant gold-ship of the very newest plan
  Was tearing chunks of pay-dirt from the shore.

It wallowed in its water-bed; it burrowed, heaved
    and swung;
  It gnawed its way ahead with grunts and sighs;
Its bill of fare was rock and sand; the tailings
    were its dung;
  It glared around with fierce electric eyes.
Full fifty buckets crammed its maw; it bellowed
    out for more;
  It looked like some great monster in the gloom.
With two to feed its sateless greed, it worked for
    seven score,
  And I sighed: "Ah, old-time miner, here's your
    doom!"

The idle windlass turns to rust; the sagging sluice-
    box falls;
  The holes you digged are water to the brim;
Your little sod-roofed cabins with the snugly moss-
    chinked walls
  Are deathly now and mouldering and dim.
The battle-field is silent where of old you fought
    it out;
  The claims you fiercely won are lost and sold;

THE PROSPECTOR

But there's a little army that they'll never put to
    rout—
  The men who simply live to seek the gold.

The men who can't remember when they learned
    to swing a pack,
  Or in what lawless land the quest began;
The solitary seeker with his grub-stake on his back,
  The restless buccaneer of pick and pan.
On the mesas of the Southland, on the tundras of
    the North,
  You will find us, changed in face but still the
    same;
And it isn't need, it isn't greed that sends us faring
    forth—
  It's the fever, it's the glory of the game.

For once you've panned the speckled sand and seen
    the bonny dust,
  Its peerless brightness blinds you like a spell;
It's little else you care about; you go because you
    must,
  And you feel that you could follow it to hell.
You'd follow it in hunger, and you'd follow it in
    cold;
  You'd follow it in solitude and pain;

THE PROSPECTOR

And when you're stiff and battened down let some•
    one whisper "Gold,"
  You're lief to rise and follow it again.

Yet look you, if I find the stuff it's just like so much
    dirt;
  I fling it to the four winds like a child.
It's wine and painted women and the things that
    do me hurt,
  Till I crawl back, beggared, broken, to the Wild.
Till I crawl back, sapped and sodden, to my grub-
    stake and my tent—
  There's a city, there's an army (hear them
    shout).
There's the gold in millions, millions, but I haven't
    got a cent;
  And oh, it's me, it's me that found it out.

It was my dream that made it good, my dream
    that made me go
  To lands of dread and death disprized of man;
But oh, I've known a glory that their hearts will
    never know,
  When I picked the first big nugget from my pan.
It's still my dream, my dauntless dream, that drives
    me forth once more
  To seek and starve and suffer in the Vast;

THE PROSPECTOR

That heaps my heart with eager hope, that glim-
     mers on before—
  My dream that will uplift me to the last.

Perhaps I am stark crazy, but there's none of you
     too sane;
  It's just a little matter of degree.
My hobby is to hunt out gold; it's fortressed in
     my brain;
  It's life and love and wife and home to me.
And I'll strike it, yes, I'll strike it; I've a hunch
     I cannot fail;
  I've a vision, I've a prompting, I've a call;
I hear the hoarse stampeding of an army on my
     trail,
  To the last, the greatest gold camp of them all.

Beyond the shark-tooth ranges sawing savage at
     the sky
  There's a lowering land no white man ever struck;
There's gold, there's gold in millions, and I'll find
     it if I die,
  And I'm going there once more to try my luck.
Maybe I'll fail—what matter?   It's a mandate, it's
     a vow;
  And when in lands of dreariness and dread
You seek the last lone frontier, far beyond your
     frontiers now,
  You will find the old prospector, silent, dead.

THE PROSPECTOR

You will find a tattered tent-pole with a ragged robe
    below it;
  You will find a rusted gold-pan on the sod;
You will find the claim I'm seeking, with my bones
    as stakes to show it;
  But I've sought the last Recorder, and He's—God.

THE BLACK SHEEP

"The aristocratic ne'er-do-well in Canada frequently finds his way into the ranks of the Royal North-West Mounted Police."—*Extract.*

Hark to the ewe that bore him:
  "*What has muddied the strain?*
Never his brothers before him
  Showed the h nt of a stain."
Hark to the tups and wethers;
  Hark to the old gray ram:
"*We're all of us white, but he's black as night,*
  And he'll never be worth a damn."

I'm up on the bally wood-pile at the back of the
    barracks yard;
"A damned disgrace to the force, sir," with a
    comrade standing guard;
Making the bluff I'm busy, doing my six months
    hard.

THE BLACK SHEEP

"Six months hard and dismissed, sir." Isn't that
      rather hell?
And all because of the liquor laws and the wiles
      of a native belle—
Some "hooch" I gave to a siwash brave who swore
      that he wouldn't tell.

At least they *say* that I did it. It's so in the town
      report.
All that I can recall is a night of revel and sport,
When I woke with a "head" in the guard-room,
      and they dragged me sick into court.

And the O. C. said: "You are guilty," and I said
      never a word;
For, hang it, you see I couldn't—I didn't know *what*
      had occurred,
And, under the circumstances, denial would be
      absurd.

But the one that cooked my bacon was Grubbe, of
      the City Patrol.
He fagged for my room at Eton, and didn't I devil
      his soul!
And now he is getting even, landing me down in
      the hole.

THE BLACK SHEEP

Plugging away on the wood-pile; doing chores
    round the square.
There goes an officer's lady—gives me a haughty
    stare—
Me that's an earl's own nephew—that is the
    hardest to bear.

To think of the poor old mater awaiting her prodi-
    gal son.
Tho' I broke her heart with my folly, I was always
    the white-haired one.
(That fatted calf that they're cooking will surely
    be overdone.)

I'll go back and yarn to the Bishop; I'll dance
    with the village belle;
I'll hand round tea to the ladies, and everything
    will be well.
Where I have been won't matter; what I have
    seen I won't tell.

I'll soar to their ken like a comet. They'll see me
    with never a stain;
But will they reform me?—far from it. We pay
    for our pleasure with pain;
But the dog will return to his vomit, the hog to
    his wallow again.

THE BLACK SHEEP

I've chewed on the rind of creation, and bitter I've
   tasted the same;
Stacked up against hell and damnation, I've man-
   aged to stay in the game;
I've had my moments of sorrow; I've had my
   seasons of shame.

That's past; when one's nature's a cracked one,
   it's too jolly hard to mend.
So long as the road is level, so long as I've cash to
   spend,
I'm bound to go to the devil, and it's all the same
   in the end.

The bugle is sounding for stables; the men troop
   off through the gloom;
An orderly laying the tables sings in the bright
   mess-room.
(I'll wash in the prison bucket, and brush with the
   prison broom.)

I'll lie in my cell and listen; I'll wish that I couldn't
   hear
The laugh and the chaff of the fellows swigging the
   canteen beer;
The nasal tone of the gramophone playing "The
   Bandolier."

THE BLACK SHEEP

And it seems to me, though it's misty, that night
    of the flowing bowl,
That the man who potlatched the whiskey and
    landed me into the hole
Was Grubbe, that unmerciful bounder, Grubbe, of the
    City Patrol.

THE TELEGRAPH OPERATOR

Say! wouldn't that be tough?
  This awful hush that hugs
And chokes one is enough
  To make a man go "bugs."

There's not a thing to do;
  I cannot sleep at night;
No wonder I'm so blue;
  Oh, for a friendly fight!
The din and rush of strife;
  A music-hall aglow;
A crowd, a city, life—
  Dear God, I miss it so!

Here, you have moped enough!
  Brace up and play the game!
But say, it's awful tough—
  Day after day the same
(I've said that twice, I bet).
  Well, there's not much to say.
I wish I had a pet,
  Or something I could play.

Cheer up! don't get so glum
  And sick of everything;
The worst is yet to come;
  God help you till the Spring.

THE TELEGRAPH OPERATOR

God shield you from the Fear;
   Teach you to laugh, not moan.
Ha! ha! it sounds so queer—
   Alone, alone, alone!

THE WOOD-CUTTER

The sky is like an envelope,
  One of those blue official things;
And, sealing it, to mock our hope,
  The moon, a silver wafer, clings.
What shall we find when death gives leave
To read—our sentence or reprieve?

I'm holding it down on God's scrap-pile, up on the
    fag-end of earth;
  O'er me a menace of mountains, a river that
    grits at my feet;
Face to face with my soul-self, weighing my life
    at its worth;
  Wondering what I was made for, here in my
    last retreat.

Last! Ah, yes, it's the finish. Have ever you heard
    a man cry?
  (Sobs that rake him and rend him, right from
    the base of the chest.)

97

THE WOOD-CUTTER

That's how I've cried, oh, so often; and now
    that my tears are dry,
  I sit in the desolate quiet and wait for the
    infinite Rest.

Rest! Well, it's restful around me; it's quiet clean
    to the core.
  The mountains pose in their ermine, in golden
    the hills are clad;
The big, blue, silt-freighted Yukon seethes by my
    cabin door,
  And I think it's only the river that keeps me
    from going mad.

By day it's a ruthless monster, a callous, insatiate
    thing,
  With oily bubble and eddy, with sudden swirling
    of breast;
By night it's a writhing Titan, sullenly murmuring,
  Ever and ever goaded, and ever crying for rest.

It cries for its human tribute, but me it will never
    drown.
  I've learned the lore of my river; my river
    obeys me well.
I hew and I launch my cordwood, and raft it to
    Dawson town,
  Where wood means wine and women, and,
    incidentally, hell.

THE WOOD-CUTTER

Hell and the anguish thereafter. Here as I sit
    alone
  I'd give the life I have left me to lighten some
    load of care:
(The bitterest part of the bitter is being denied to
    atone;
Lips that have mocked at Heaven lend them-
    selves ill to prayer.)

Impotent as a beetle pierced on the needle of Fate;
  A wretch in a cosmic death-cell, peaks for my prison
    bars;
'Whelmed by a world stupendous, lonely and listless
    I wait,
  Drowned in a sea of silence, strewn with confetti
    of stars.

See! from far up the valley a rapier pierces the
    night,
  The white search-ray of a steamer. Swiftly,
    serenely it nears;
A proud, white, alien presence, a glittering galley
    of light,
  Confident-poised, triumphant, freighted with
    hopes and fears.

I look as one looks on a vision; I see it pulsating by;
  I glimpse joy-radiant faces; I hear the thresh
    of the wheel.

THE WOOD-CUTTER

Hoof-like my heart beats a moment; then silence
    swoops from the sky.
  Darkness is piled upon darkness. God only
    knows how I feel.

Maybe you've seen me sometimes; maybe you've
    pitied me then—
  The lonely waif of the wood-camp, here by my
    cabin door.
Some day you'll look and see not; futile and out-
    cast of men,
  I shall be far from your pity, resting forevermore.

My life was a problem in ciphers, a weary and
    profitless sum.
  Slipshod and stupid I worked it, dazed by negation
    and doubt.
Ciphers the total confronts me. Oh, Death, with thy
    moistened thumb,
  Stoop like a petulant schoolboy, wipe me forever out!

THE SONG OF THE MOUTH-ORGAN

(With apologies to the singer of the "Song of the Banjo.")

I'm a homely little bit of tin and bone;
   I'm beloved by the Legion of the Lost;
I haven't got a "vox humana" tone,
   And a dime or two will satisfy my cost.
I don't attempt your high-falutin' flights;
   I am more or less uncertain on the key;
But I tell you, boys, there's lots and lots of nights
   When you've taken mighty comfort out of me.

I weigh an ounce or two, and I'm so small
   You can pack me in the pocket of your vest;
And when at night so wearily you crawl
   Into your bunk and stretch your limbs to rest,
You take me out and play me soft and low,
   The simple songs that trouble your heartstrings:
The tunes you used to fancy long ago,
   Before you made a rotten mess of things.

THE SONG OF THE MOUTH-ORGAN

Then a dreamy look will come into your eyes,
    And you break off in the middle of a note;
And then, with just the dreariest of sighs,
    You drop me in the pocket of your coat.
But somehow I have bucked you up a bit;
    And, as you turn around and face the wall,
You don't feel quite so spineless and unfit—
    You're not so bad a fellow after all.

Do you recollect the bitter Arctic night;
    Your camp beside the canyon on the trail;
Your tent a tiny square of orange light;
    The moon above consumptive-like and pale;
Your supper cooked, your little stove aglow;
    You tired, but snug and happy as a child?
Then 'twas "Turkey in the Straw" till your lips
            were nearly raw,
    And you hurled your bold defiance at the Wild

Do you recollect the flashing, lashing pain;
    The gulf of humid blackness overhead;
The lightning making rapiers of the rain;
    The cattle-horns like candles of the dead
You sitting on your bronco there alone,
    In your slicker, saddle-sore and sick with cold?
Do you think the silent herd did not hear "The
            Mocking Bird,"
    Or relish "Silver Threads among the Gold?"

THE SONG OF THE MOUTH-ORGAN

Do you recollect the wild Magellan coast;
    The head-winds and the icy, roaring seas;
The nights you thought that everything was lost;
    The days you toiled in water to your knees;
The frozen ratlines shrieking in the gale;
    The hissing steeps and gulfs of livid foam:
When you cheered your messmates nine with "Ben
        Bolt" and "Clementine,"
    And "Dixie Land" and "Seeing Nellie Home?"

Let the jammy banjo voice the Younger Son,
    Who waits for his remittance to arrive;
I represent the grimy, gritty one,
    Who sweats his bones to keep himself alive;
Who's up against the real thing from his birth;
    Whose heritage is hard and bitter toil;
I voice the weary, smeary ones of earth,
    The helots of the sea and of the soil.

I'm the Steinway of strange mischief and mischance;
    I'm the Stradivarius of blank defeat;
In the down-world, when the devil leads the dance,
    I am simply and symbolically meet;
I'm the irrepressive spirit of mankind;
    I'm the small boy playing knuckle down with
        Death;
At the end of all things known, where God's rubbish-
        heap is thrown,
    I shrill impudent triumph at a breath.

THE SONG OF THE MOUTH-ORGAN

I'm a humble little bit of tin and horn;
  I'm a byword, I'm a plaything, I'm a jest;
The virtuoso looks on me with scorn;
  But there's times when I am better than the
    best.
Ask the stoker and the sailor of the sea;
  Ask the mucker and the hewer of the pine;
Ask the herder of the plain, ask the gleaner of the
      grain—
  There's a lowly, loving kingdom—and it's mine.

THE TRAIL OF NINETY-EIGHT

I

Gold! We leapt from our benches. Gold! We
sprang from our stools.
Gold! We wheeled in the furrow, fired with the
faith of fools.
Fearless, unfound, unfitted, far from the night and
the cold,
Heard we the clarion summons, followed the master-
lure—Gold!

Men from the sands of the Sunland; men from the
woods of the West;
Men from the farms and the cities, into the North-
land we pressed.
Graybeards and striplings and women, good men
and bad men and bold,
Leaving our homes and our loved ones, crying
exultantly—"Gold!"

Never was seen such an army, pitiful, futile, unfit;
Never was seen such a spirit, manifold courage and
grit

THE TRAIL OF NINETY-EIGHT

Never has been such a cohort under one banner
    unrolled
As surged to the ragged-edged Arctic, urged by
    the arch-tempter—Gold.

"Farewell!" we cried to our dearests; little we
    cared for their tears.
"Farewell!" we cried to the humdrum and the yoke
    of the hireling years;
Just like a pack of school-boys, and the big crowd
    cheered us good-bye.
Never were hearts so uplifted, never were hopes so
    high.

The spectral shores flitted past us, and every whirl
    of the screw
Hurled us nearer to fortune, and ever we planned
    what we'd do—
Do with the gold when we got it—big, shiny
    nuggets like plums,
There in the sand of the river, gouging it out with
    our thumbs.

And one man wanted a castle, another a racing
    stud;
A third would cruise in a palace yacht like a red-
    necked prince of blood.

THE TRAIL OF NINETY-EIGHT

And so we dreamed and we vaunted, millionaires
    to a man,
Leaping to wealth in our visions long ere the trail
    began.

II.

We landed in wind-swept Skagway. We joined
    the weltering mass,
Clamoring over their outfits, waiting to climb the
    Pass.
We tightened our girths and our pack-straps; we
    linked on the Human Chain,
Struggling up to the summit, where every step was
    a pain.

Gone was the joy of our faces, grim and haggard
    and pale;
The heedless mirth of the shipboard was changed
    to the care of the trail.
We flung ourselves in the struggle, packing our
    grub in relays,
Step by step to the summit in the bale of the winter
    days.

Floundering deep in the sump-holes, stumbling out
    again;
Crying with cold and weakness, crazy with fear and
    pain.

THE TRAIL OF NINETY-EIGHT

Then from the depths of our travail, ere our spirits
    were broke,
Grim, tenacious and savage, the lust of the trail
    awoke.

"Klondike or bust!" rang the slogan; every man
    for his own.
Oh, how we flogged the horses, staggering skin and
    bone!
Oh, how we cursed their weakness, anguish they
    could not tell,
Breaking their hearts in our passion, lashing them
    on till they fell!

For grub meant gold to our thinking, and all that
    could walk must pack;
The sheep for the shambles stumbled, each with a
    load on its back;
And even the swine were burdened, and grunted
    and squealed and rolled,
And men went mad in the moment, huskily clam-
    oring "Gold!"

Oh, we were brutes and devils, goaded by lust and
    fear!
Our eyes were strained to the summit; the weak-
    lings dropped to the rear,

THE TRAIL OF NINETY-EIGHT

Falling in heaps by the trail-side, heart-broken,
   limp and wan;
But the gaps closed up in an instant, and heedless
   the chain went on.

Never will I forget it, there on the mountain face,
Antlike, men with their burdens, clinging in icy
   space;
Dogged, determined and dauntless, cruel and cal-
   lous and cold,
Cursing, blaspheming, reviling, and ever that battle-
   cry—"Gold!"

Thus toiled we, the army of fortune, in hunger and
   hope and despair,
Till glacier, mountain and forest vanished, and,
   radiantly fair,
There at our feet lay Lake Bennett, and down to
   its welcome we ran:
The trail of the land was over, the trail of the water
   began.

III.

We built our boats and we launched them.   Never
   has been such a fleet;
A packing-case for a bottom, a mackinaw for a sheet.
Shapeless, grotesque, lopsided, flimsy, makeshift
   and crude,
Each man after his fashion builded as best he could.

THE TRAIL OF NINETY-EIGHT

Each man worked like a demon, as prow to rudder
 we raced;
The winds of the Wild cried "Hurry!" the voice of
 the waters, "Haste!"
We hated those driving before us; we dreaded
 those pressing behind;
We cursed the slow current that bore us; we prayed
 to the God of the wind.

Spring! and the hillsides flourished, vivid in jew-
 elled green;
Spring! and our hearts' blood nourished envy and
 hatred and spleen.
Little cared we for the Spring-birth; much cared
 we to get on—
Stake in the Great White Channel, stake ere the
 best be gone.

The greed of the gold possessed us; pity and love
 were forgot;
Covetous visions obsessed us; brother with brother
 fought.
Partner with partner wrangled, each one claiming
 his due;
Wrangled and halved their outfits, sawing their
 boats in two.

THE TRAIL OF NINETY-EIGHT

Thuswise we voyaged Lake Bennett, Tagish,
    then Windy Arm,
Sinister, savage and baleful, boding us hate and
    harm.
Many a scow was shattered there on that iron
    shore;
Many a heart was broken straining at sweep and
    oar.

We roused Lake Marsh with a chorus, we drifted
    many a mile;
There was the canyon before us—cave-like its
    dark defile;
The shores swept faster and faster; the river nar-
    rowed to wrath;
Waters that hissed disaster reared upright in our
    path.

Beneath us the green tumult churning, above us
    the cavernous gloom;
Around us, swift twisting and turning, the black,
    sullen walls of a tomb.
We spun like a chip in a mill-race; our hearts ham-
    mered under the test;
Then—oh, the relief on each chill face!—we soared
    into sunlight and rest.

THE TRAIL OF NINETY-EIGHT

Hand sought for hand on the instant. Cried we,
    "Our troubles are o'er!"
Then, like a rumble of thunder, heard we a canorous
    roar.
Leaping and boiling and seething, saw we a cauldron
    afume;
There was the rage of the rapids, there was the
    menace of doom.

The river springs like a racer, sweeps through a
    gash in the rock;
Buts at the boulder-ribbed bottom, staggers and
    rears at the shock;
Leaps like a terrified monster, writhes in its fury
    and pain;
Then with the crash of a demon springs to the
    onset again.

Dared we that ravening terror; heard we its din
    in our ears;
Called on the Gods of our fathers, juggled forlorn
    with our fears;
Sank to our waists in its fury, tossed to the sky
    like a fleece;
Then, when our dread was the greatest, crashed
    into safety and peace.

THE TRAIL OF NINETY-EIGHT

But what of the others that followed, losing their
    boats by the score?
Well could we see them and hear them, strung
    down that desolate shore.
What of the poor souls that perished? Little of
    them shall be said—
On to the Golden Valley, pause not to bury the
    dead.

Then there were days of drifting, breezes soft as a
    sigh;
Night trailed her robe of jewels over the floor of
    the sky.
The moonlit stream was a python, silver, sinuous,
    vast,
That writhed on a shroud of velvet—well, it was
    done at last.

There were the tents of Dawson, there the scar of
    the slide;
Swiftly we poled o'er the shallows, swiftly leapt
    o'er the side.
Fires fringed the mouth of Bonanza; sunset gilded
    the dome;
The test of the trail was over—thank God, thank
    God, we were Home!

THE BALLAD OF GUM-BOOT BEN

*He was an old prospector with a vision bleared and
    dim.*
*He asked me for a grubstake, and the same I gave
    to him.*
*He hinted of a hidden trove, and when I made so
    bold*
To question his veracity, this is the tale he told.

"I do not seek the copper streak, nor yet the
    yellow dust;
I am not fain for sake of gain to irk the frozen
    crust;
Let fellows gross find gilded dross, far other is my
    mark;
Oh, gentle youth, this is the truth—I go to seek
    the Ark.

"I prospected the Pelly bed, I prospected the
    White;
The Nordenscold for love of gold I piked from
    morn till night;

THE BALLAD OF GUM-BOOT BEN

Afar and near for many a year I led the wild
      stampede,
Until I guessed that all my quest was vanity and
      greed.

"Then came I to a land I knew no man had ever
      seen,
A haggard land, forlornly spanned by mountains
      lank and lean;
The nitchies said 'twas full of dread, of smoke and
      fiery breath,
And no man dare put foot in there for fear of pain
      and death.

"But I was made all unafraid, so, careless and alone,
Day after day I made my way into that land
      unknown;
Night after night by camp-fire light I crouched in
      lonely thought;
Oh, gentle youth, this is the truth—I knew not
      what I sought.

"I rose at dawn; I wandered on. 'Tis somewhat
      fine and grand
To be alone and hold your own in God's vast
      awesome land;

THE BALLAD OF GUM-BOOT BEN

Come woe or weal, 'tis fine to feel a hundred
    miles between
The trails you dare and pathways where the feet
    of men have been.

"And so it fell on me a spell of wander-lust was
    cast.
The land was still and strange and chill, and
    cavernous and vast;
And sad and dead, and dull as lead, the valleys
    sought the snows;
And far and wide on every side the ashen peaks
    arose.

"The moon was like a silent spike that pierced
    the sky right through;
The small stars popped and winked and hopped
    in vastitudes of blue;
And unto me for company came creatures of the
    shade,
And formed in rings and whispered things that
    made me half afraid.

"And strange though be, 'twas borne on me that
    land had lived of old,
And men had crept and slain and slept where now
    they toiled for gold;

THE BALLAD OF GUM-BOOT BEN

Through jungles dim the mammoth grim had
    sought the oozy fen,
And on his track, all bent of back, had crawled the
    hairy men.

"And furthermore, strange deeds of yore in this
    dead place were done.
They haunted me, as wild and free I roamed from
    sun to sun;
Until I came where sudden flame uplit a terraced
    height,
A regnant peak that seemed to seek the coronal
    of night.

"I scaled the peak; my heart was weak, yet on
    and on I pressed.
Skyward I strained until I gained its dazzling
    silver crest;
And there I found, with all around a world supine
    and stark,
Swept clean of snow, a flat plateau, and on it
    lay—the Ark.

"Yes, there, I knew, by two and two the beasts did
    disembark,
And so in haste I ran and traced in letters on the
    Ark

117

THE BALLAD OF GUM-BOOT BEN

My human name—Ben Smith's the same. And
    now I want to float
A syndicate to haul and freight to town that noble
    boat."

I met him later in a bar and made a gay remark
Anent an ancient miner and an option on the Ark.
He gazed at me reproachfully, as only topers can;
But what he said I can't repeat—he was a bad old
    man.

CLANCY OF THE MOUNTED POLICE

In the little Crimson Manual it's written plain
    and clear
That who would wear the scarlet coat shall say
    good-bye to fear;
Shall be a guardian of the right, a sleuth-hound of
    the trail—
In the little Crimson Manual there's no such word
    as "fail"—
Shall follow on though heavens fall, or hell's top-
    turrets freeze,
Half round the world, if need there be, on bleeding
    hands and knees.
It's duty, duty, first and last, the Crimson Manual
    saith;
The Scarlet Rider makes reply: "It's duty—to
    the death."
And so they sweep the solitudes, free men from all
    the earth;
And so they sentinel the woods, the wilds that
    know their worth;
And so they scour the startled plains and mock
    at hurt and pain,

CLANCY OF THE MOUNTED POLICE

And read their Crimson Manual, and find their
duty plain.
Knights of the lists of unrenown, born of the
frontier's need,
Disdainful of the spoken word, exultant in the
deed;
Unconscious heroes of the waste, proud players
of the game,
Props of the power behind the throne, upholders
of the name:
For thus the Great White Chief hath said, "In
all my lands be peace,"
And to maintain his word he gave his West the
Scarlet Police.

Livid-lipped was the valley, still as the grave of
God;
    Misty shadows of mountain thinned into mists
of cloud;
Corpselike and stark was the land, with a quiet
that crushed and awed,
    And the stars of the weird sub-arctic glimmered
over its shroud.

Deep in the trench of the valley two men stationed
the Post,
    Seymour and Clancy the reckless, fresh from
the long patrol;

CLANCY OF THE MOUNTED POLICE

Seymour, the sergeant, and Clancy—Clancy who
made his boast
He could cinch like a bronco the Northland,
and cling to the prongs of the Pole.

Two lone men on detachment, standing for law
on the trail;
Undismayed in the vastness, wise with the
wisdom of old—
Out of the night hailed a half-breed telling a pitiful
tale,
"White man starving and crazy on the banks
of the Nordenscold."

Up sprang the red-haired Clancy, lean and eager
of eye;
Loaded the long toboggan, strapped each dog
at its post;
Whirled his lash at the leader; then, with a whoop
and a cry,
Into the Great White Silence faded away like
a ghost.

The clouds were a misty shadow, the hills were
a shadowy mist;
Sunless, voiceless and pulseless, the day was a
dream of woe;

CLANCY OF THE MOUNTED POLICE

Through the ice-rifts the river smoked and bubbled
and hissed;
  Behind was a trail fresh broken, in front the un-
  trodden snow.

Ahead of the dogs ploughed Clancy, haloed by
steaming breath;
  Through peril of open water, through ache of
  insensate cold;
Up rivers wantonly winding in a land affianced
to death,
  Till he came to a cowering cabin on the banks
  of the Nordenscold.

Then Clancy loosed his revolver, and he strode
through the open door;
  And there was the man he sought for, crouching
  beside the fire;
The hair of his beard was singeing, the frost on his
back was hoar,
  And ever he crooned and chanted as if he never
  would tire:—

*"I panned and I panned in the shiny sand, and I
sniped on the river bar;*
*But I know, I know, that it's down below that
the golden treasures are;*

122

CLANCY OF THE MOUNTED POLICE

So I'll wait and wait till the floods abate, and I'll
sink a shaft once more,
And I'd like to bet that I'll go home yet with a
brass band playing before."

He was nigh as thin as a sliver, and he whined like
a Moose-hide cur;
So Clancy clothed him and nursed him as a
mother nurses a child;
Lifted him on the toboggan, wrapped him in robes
of fur,
Then with the dogs sore straining started to
face the Wild.

Said the Wild, "I will crush this Clancy, so fearless
and insolent;
For him will I loose my fury, and blind and
buffet and beat;
Pile up my snows to stay him; then when his
strength is spent,
Leap on him from my ambush and crush him
under my feet.

"Him will I ring with my silence, compass him
with my cold;
Closer and closer clutch him unto mine icy
breast;

CLANCY OF THE MOUNTED POLICE

Buffet him with my blizzards, deep in my snows
    enfold,
  Claiming his life as my tribute, giving my
    wolves the rest."

Clancy crawled through the vastness; o'er him
    the hate of the Wild;
  Full on his face fell the blizzard; cheering his
    huskies he ran;
Fighting, fierce-hearted and tireless, snows that
    drifted and piled,
  With ever and ever behind him singing the
    crazy man.

> *"Sing hey, sing ho, for the ice and snow,*
> *And a heart that's ever merry;*
> *Let us trim and square with a lover's care*
> *(For why should a man be sorry?)*
> *A grave deep, deep, with the moon a-peep,*
> *A grave in the frozen mould.*
> *Sing hey, sing ho, for the winds that blow,*
> *And a grave deep down in the ice and snow,*
> *A grave in the land of gold."*

Day after day of darkness, the whirl of the seeth-
    ing snows;
  Day after day of blindness, the swoop of the
    stinging blast;

CLANCY OF THE MOUNTED POLICE

On through a blur of fury the swing of staggering
    blows;
  On through a world of turmoil, empty, inane
    and vast.

Night with its writhing storm-whirl, night des-
    pairingly black;
  Night with its hours of terror, numb and end-
    lessly long;
Night with its weary waiting, fighting the shadows
    back,
  And ever the crouching madman singing his
    crazy song.

Cold with its creeping terror, cold with its sudden
    clinch;
  Cold so utter you wonder if 'twill ever again be
    warm;
Clancy grinned as he shuddered, "Surely it isn't
    a cinch
  Being wet-nurse to a looney in the teeth of an
    arctic storm."

The blizzard passed and the dawn broke, knife-
    edged and crystal clear;
  The sky was a blue-domed iceberg, sunshine
    outlawed away;

CLANCY OF THE MOUNTED POLICE

Ever by snowslide and ice-rip haunted and hovered
    the Fear;
  Ever the Wild malignant poised and panted to
    slay.

The lead-dog freezes in harness—cut him out of
    the team!
  The lung of the wheel-dog's bleeding—shoot
    him and let him lie!
On and on with the others—lash them until they
    scream!
  "Pull for your lives, you devils! On! To halt
    is to die."

There in the frozen vastness Clancy fought with
    his foes;
  The ache of the stiffened fingers, the cut of the
    snowshoe thong;
Cheeks black-raw through the hood-flap, eyes that
    tingled and closed,
  And ever to urge and cheer him quavered the
    madman's song.

Colder it grew and colder, till the last heat left the
    earth,
  And there in the great stark stillness the bale
    fires glinted and gleamed,

CLANCY OF THE MOUNTED POLICE

And the Wild all around exulted and shook with
 a devilish mirth,
  And life was far and forgotten, the ghost of a
  joy once dreamed.

Death! And one who defied it, a man of the
 Mounted Police;
  Fought it there to a standstill long after hope
  was gone;
Grinned through his bitter anguish, fought with-
 out let or cease,
  Suffering, straining, striving, stumbling, strug-
  gling on.

Till the dogs lay down in their traces, and rose and
 staggered and fell;
  Till the eyes of him dimmed with shadows, and
  the trail was so hard to see;
Till the Wild howled out triumphant, and the
 world was a frozen hell—
  Then said Constable Clancy: "I guess that it's
  up to me."

Far down the trail they saw him, and his hands
 they were blanched like bone;
  His face was a blackened horror, from his eye-
  lids the salt rheum ran;

CLANCY OF THE MOUNTED POLICE

His feet he was lifting strangely, as if they were
    made of stone,
  But safe in his arms and sleeping he carried
    the crazy man.

So Clancy got into Barracks, and the boys made
    rather a scene;
  And the O. C. called him a hero, and was nice
    as a man could be;
But Clancy gazed down his trousers at the place
    where his toes had been,
  And then he howled like a husky, and sang in
    a shaky key:

"*When I go back to the old love that's true to the
    finger-tips,*
*I'll say: 'Here's bushels of gold, love,' and I'll kiss
    my girl on the lips;*
*'It's yours to have and to hold, love.' It's the proud,
    proud boy I'll be,*
*When I go back to the old love that's waited so long
    for me.*"

LOST

"Black is the sky, but the land is white—
(O the wind, the snow and the storm!)—
Father, where is our boy to-night?
Pray to God he is safe and warm."

"Mother, mother, why should you fear?
Safe is he, and the Arctic moon
Over his cabin shines so clear—
Rest and sleep, 'twill be morning soon."

"It's getting dark awful sudden. Say, this is
   mighty queer!
   Where in the world have I got to? It's still
   and black as a tomb.
I reckoned the camp was yonder, I figured the
   trail was here—
   Nothing! Just draw and valley packed with
   quiet and gloom;

LOST

Snow that comes down like feathers, thick and
    gobby and gray;
Night that looks spiteful ugly—seems that I've
    lost my way.

"The cold's got an edge like a jackknife—it must
    be forty below;
  Leastways that's what it seems like—it cuts so
    fierce to the bone.
The wind's getting real ferocious; it's heaving and
    whirling the snow;
  It shrieks with a howl of fury, it dies away to
    a moan;
Its arms sweep round like a banshee's, swift and
    icily white,
And buffet and blind and beat me.   Lord! it's
    a hell of a night.

"I'm all tangled up in a blizzard. There's only
    one thing to do—
  Keep on moving and moving; it's death, it's
    death if I rest.
Oh, God! if I see the morning, if only I struggle
    through,
  I'll say the prayers I've forgotten since I lay on
    my mother's breast.
I seem going round in a circle; maybe the camp is
    near.

LOST

Say! did somebody holler? Was it a light I
    saw?
Or was it only a notion? I'll shout, and maybe
    they'll hear—
  No! the wind only drowns me—shout till my
    throat is raw.

"The boys are all round the camp-fire wondering
    when I'll be back.
  They'll soon be starting to seek me; they'll
    scarcely wait for the light.
What will they find, I wonder, when they come to
    the end of my track—
  A hand stuck out of a snowdrift, frozen and
    stiff and white.
That's what they'll strike, I reckon; that's how
    they'll find their pard,
  A pie-faced corpse in a snowbank—curse you,
    don't be a fool!
Play the game to the finish; bet on your very last
    card;
  Nerve yourself for the struggle. Oh, you coward,
    keep cool!

"I'm going to lick this blizzard; I'm going to live
    the night.
  It can't down me with its bluster—I'm not the
    kind to be beat.

LOST

On hands and knees will I buck it; with every
    breath will I fight;
    It's life, it's life that I fight for—never it seemed
      so sweet.
I know that my face is frozen; my hands are
    numblike and dead;
    But oh, my feet keep a-moving, heavy and hard
      and slow;
They're trying to kill me, kill me, the night that's
    black overhead,
    The wind that cuts like a razor, the whipcord
      lash of the snow.
Keep a-moving, a-moving; don't, don't stumble,
    you fool!
    Curse this snow that's a-piling a-purpose to
      block my way.
It's heavy as gold in the rocker, it's white and
    fleecy as wool;
    It's soft as a bed of feathers, it's warm as a
      stack of hay.
Curse on my feet that slip so, my poor tired,
    stumbling feet—
    I guess they're a job for the surgeon, they feel
      so queerlike to lift—
I'll rest them just for a moment—oh, but to rest
    is sweet!
    The awful wind cannot get me, deep, deep down
      in the drift."

LOST

" Father, a bitter cry I heard,
  Out of the night so dark and wild.
Why is my heart so strangely stirred?
  'Twas like the voice of our erring child."

" Mother, mother, you only heard
  A waterfowl in the locked lagoon—
Out of the night a wounded bird—
  Rest and sleep, 'twill be morning soon."

Who is it talks of sleeping? I'll swear that some-
    body shook
  Me hard by the arm for a moment, but how on
    earth could it be?
See how my feet are moving—awfully funny they
    look—
  Moving as if they belonged to a someone that
    wasn't me.
The wind down the night's long alley bowls me
    down like a pin;
  I stagger and fall and stagger, crawl arm-deep
    in the snow.
Beaten back to my corner, how can I hope to win?
  And there is the blizzard waiting to give me the
    knockout blow.

Oh, I'm so warm and sleepy! No more hunger and
    pain.
  Just to rest for a moment; was ever rest such
    a joy?

133

LOST

Ha! what was that? I'll swear it, somebody
    shook me again;
  Somebody seemed to whisper: "Fight to the
    last, my boy."
Fight! That's right, I must struggle. I know
    that to rest means death;
  Death, but then what does death mean?—ease
    from a world of strife.
Life has been none too pleasant; yet with my
    failing breath
  Still and still must I struggle, fight for the gift
    of life.

    *   *   *   *   *   *

Seems that I must be dreaming! Here is the old
    home trail;
  Yonder a light is gleaming; oh, I know it so well!
The air is scented with clover; the cattle wait by
    the rail;
  Father is through with the milking; there goes
    the supper-bell.

    *   *   *   *   *   *

Mother, your boy is crying, out in the night and
    cold;
  Let me in and forgive me, I'll never be bad
    any more:

LOST

I'm, oh, so sick and so sorry: please, dear mother,
    don't scold—
It's just your boy, and he wants you. . . .
    Mother, open the door. . . .

" Father, father, I saw a face
*   Pressed just now to the window-pane!*
Oh, it gazed for a moment's space,
*   Wild and wan, and was gone again!"*

" Mother, mother, you saw the snow
*   Drifted down from the maple tree*
(Oh, the wind that is sobbing so!
*   Weary and worn and old are we)—*
Only the snow and a wounded loon—
Rest and sleep, 'twill be morning soon."

L'ENVOI

We talked of yesteryears, of trails and treasure,
 Of men who played the game and lost or won;
Of mad stampedes, of toil beyond all measure,
 Of camp-fire comfort when the day was done.
We talked of sullen nights by moon-dogs haunted,
 Of bird and beast and tree, of rod and gun;
Of boat and tent, of hunting-trip enchanted
 Beneath the wonder of the midnight sun;
Of bloody-footed dogs that gnawed the traces,
 Of prisoned seas, wind-lashed and winter-locked;
The ice-gray dawn was pale upon our faces,
 Yet still we filled the cup and still we talked.

The city street was dimmed.   We saw the glitter
 Of moon-picked brilliants on the virgin snow,
And down the drifted canyon heard the bitter,
 Relentless slogan of the winds of woe.
The city was forgot, and, parka-skirted,
 We trod that leagueless land that once we knew;

L'ENVOI

We saw stream past, down valleys glacier-girted,
  The wolf-worn legions of the caribou.
We smoked our pipes, o'er scenes of triumph dwelling;
  Of deeds of daring, dire defeats, we talked;
And other tales that lost not in the telling,
  Ere to our beds uncertainly we walked.

And so, dear friends, in gentler valleys roaming,
  Perhaps, when on my printed page you look,
Your fancies by the firelight may go homing
  To that lone land that haply you forsook.
And if perchance you hear the silence calling,
  The frozen music of star-yearning heights,
Or, dreaming, see the seines of silver trawling
  Across the sky's abyss on vasty nights,
You may recall that sweep of savage splendor,
  That land that measures each man at his worth,
And feel in memory, half fierce, half tender,
  The brotherhood of men that know the North.